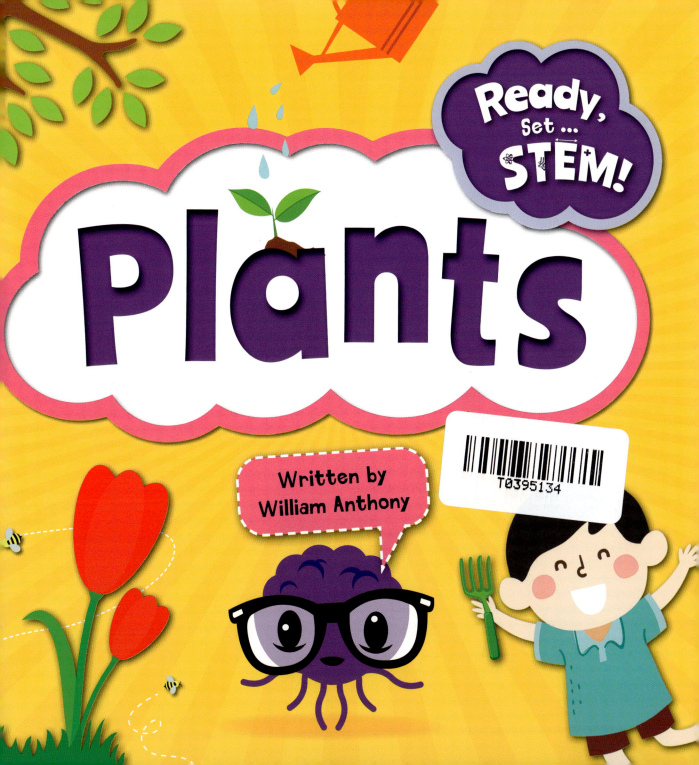

North American adaptation copyright © 2025 by North Star Editions, Mendota Heights, MN 55120. All rights reserved. No part of this book may be reproduced or utilized in any form or by any means without written permission from the publisher.
Plants © 2021 BookLife Publishing
This edition is published by arrangement with BookLife Publishing

sales@northstareditions.com | 888-417-0195

Library of Congress Control Number:
The Library of Congress Control Number is available on the Library of Congress website.

ISBN
979-8-89359-291-7 (library bound)
979-8-89359-296-2 (paperback)
979-8-89359-305-1 (epub)
979-8-89359-301-3 (hosted ebook)

Printed in the United States of America
Mankato, MN

012025

Written by
William Anthony
Edited by:
Robin Twiddy
Designed by:
Amy Li

All facts, statistics, web addresses and URLs in this book were verified as valid and accurate at time of writing. No responsibility for any changes to external websites or references can be accepted by either the author or publisher.

Photo Credits

Images are courtesy of Shutterstock.com. With thanks to Getty Images, Thinkstock Photo, and iStockphoto.

Recurring images – Micra (brain, sunburst pattern), Lorelyn Medina (children vectors), illustrator096 (clouds), MicroOne (line of flowers), Pogorelova Olga (grass). Cover–p1 – Anna Frajitova, melaics, Oxy_gen, Vasenina Daria, p2–3 – Patrick Foto, Oxy_gen, Anna Frajitova, p4–5 – LuckyVector, Illonajalll, Makistock, melaics, StevanZZ, Lorelyn Medina, p6–7 – stockakia, venimo, GOLFX, p8–9 – melaics, Africa Studio, Vasenina Daria, p10–11 – AlexTanya, Lidiane Miotto, p12–13 – vladwel, Anna Frajtova, p14–15 – Lorelyn Medina, Tijana Simic, Ksusha Dusmikeeva, AnnaKoro, p16–17 – Travel Faery, Denis Kuvaev, p18–19 – Infinity, Maks Narodenko, Ternavskaia Olga Alibec, p20–21 – Alexander Lysenko, Ksusha Dusmikeeva, p22–24 – AlexTanya, Jacob Lund, Prettyawesome, Anna Frajtova.

Contents

Page 4	A Planet of Plants
Page 6	Types of Plant
Page 8	Super Seeds
Page 10	Remarkable Roots
Page 12	Splendid Stems
Page 14	Lovely Leaves
Page 16	Fabulous Flowers
Page 18	Fantastic Fruit
Page 20	Create Your Own
Page 22	Take a Trip
Page 24	Glossary and Index

Words that look like this can be found in the glossary on page 24.

Plants are living things. They need water and air to live. What other things can you think of that are alive?

Ready, Set ... THINK!

Types of Plants

There are many types of plants. They can be tall or short. They can have lots of different colors. Trees, flowers, and <u>weeds</u> are all plants.

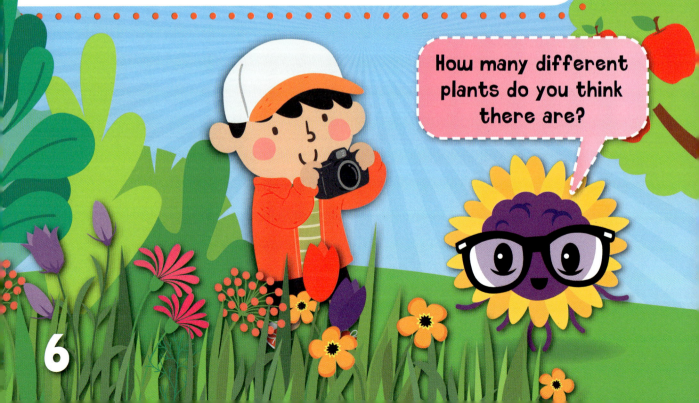

How many different plants do you think there are?

Take a walk outside with an adult. How many different types of plants can you count? Most plants grow in soil in the ground.

Ready, Set ... COUNT!

Super Seeds

Many plants start as seeds or <u>bulbs</u>. Seeds can be very small. A whole plant will grow from one seed or bulb.

Ask an adult if you can grow a plant at home or at school. Dig up some soil and put the seed in.

Ready, Set... DIG!

Remarkable Roots

Seeds need water to grow. When the seed has the right conditions, it will start to grow roots.

Roots help keep the plant in place.

Roots

Once the roots have grown, they will take in water for the plant. Let's water the seed you planted to help it grow!

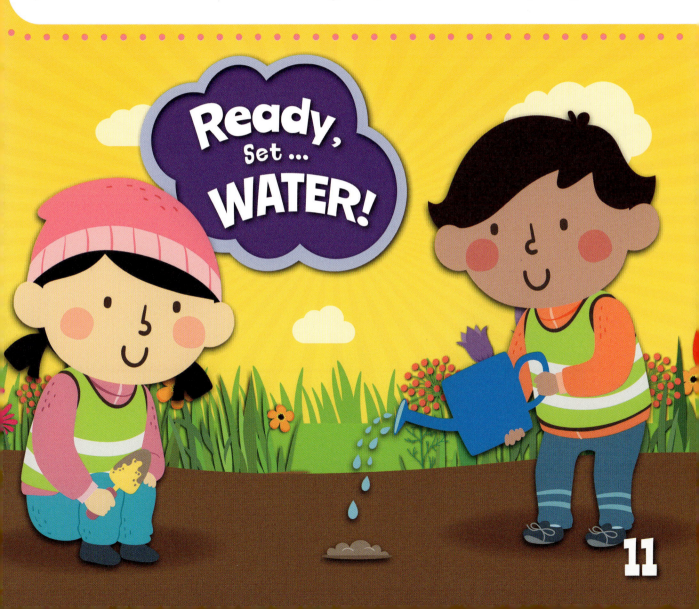

Splendid Stems

The tall part of the plant that grows out of the soil is called a stem. This is where water and <u>nutrients</u> move through the plant.

Trees have large, wooden stems called trunks. You can usually tell the age of a tree by the number of rings in the trunk. Can you count how old this tree is?

Ready, Set ... COUNT!

Each ring is one year.

Answer: The tree is six (6) years old.

Lovely Leaves

Leaves can be different shapes and sizes. Some leaves change color from green to orange, red, or yellow at different times of the year.

Let's make some leaf art!

Fabulous Flowers

Some plants have flowers. They can be bright and colorful, smell wonderful, and be all different shapes and sizes.

This field smells amazing!

See if you can find a flower to smell. Then, try to <u>describe</u> its smell using three different words.

Ready, Set ... SNIFF!

Fantastic Fruit

Some flowers turn into fruit. The seeds of a plant are in its fruit. If these seeds end up in the ground, they can grow into a new plant.

Can you spot the seeds inside this apple?

18

We can eat some fruits when they are <u>ripe</u>. Grab two types of fruit, such as a slice of watermelon and a strawberry. Taste them and try to describe the difference.

Create Your Own

Can you create your own amazing plant? Grab a pencil and start drawing. Label all of its parts.

Will it be taller than 100 humans?

Will it grow <u>multicolored</u> fruit?

Will it have a curly stem?

Will it have beautiful flowers?

Ready, Set... DRAW!

Take a Trip

If you want to see lots of flowers, why not visit a flower show? There are lots of flowers to see.

You could also visit a forest. While you are there, you could see how many different types of plants you can count.

Ready, Set ... EXPLORE!

Glossary

bulbs	rounded parts of some plants that are under the ground and grow into new plants
conditions	the state of the environment, such as the temperature and wetness
describe	to say what something is like
multicolored	made up of lots of different colors
nutrients	things that plants and animals need to grow and stay healthy
ripe	fully grown and ready to be eaten
weeds	plants that grow very quickly where they are not wanted

Index

bulbs, 8
eating, 19
flowers, 6, 16–18, 21–22
fruits, 18–19, 21
leaves, 14–15, 20
roots, 10–11

seeds, 8–11, 18
soil, 7, 9, 12
stems, 12–13, 21
trunks, 13
water, 5, 10–12